# Teaching Fido to Learn to Earn

### Dr. Yin's Program for Developing Leadership in Humans and Impulse Control in Dogs

## Dr. Sophia Yin, DVM, MS

### With Illustrations by Lili Chin

**Teaching Fido to Learn to Earn:**
Dr. Yin's Program for Developing Leadership in Humans and Impulse Control in Dogs

by Dr. Sophia Yin, DVM, MS

Copyright 2012 by Sophia A. Yin
ISBN: 978-0-9641518-7-1

Graphic Designers: Larry Peters and April Kimmerly
Illustrator: Lili Chin (www.doggiedrawing.net)

Disclaimer
The publisher and the author make no representation or warranties with respect to the accuracy or completeness of the contents of this work and specifically disclaim all warranties, including without limitation warranties of fitness for a particular purpose. No warranty may be created or extended by sales or promotional materials. The advice and strategies contained herein may not be suitable for every situation. This work is sold with the understanding that the publisher is not engaged in rendering legal, veterinary, or other professional services. If professional assistance is required, the services of a competent professional person should be sought. Neither the publisher nor the author shall be liable for damages arising heretofore. The fact that an organization or website is referred to in this work as a citation and/or a potential source of further information does not mean that the author or the publisher endorses the information that the organization or website may produce or recommendations it may make. Further, readers should be aware that websites listed in this work may have changed or disappeared between when this work was written and when it was read.

For free pet-care and pet-behavior information, as well as to view other products by Dr. Sophia Yin, go to www.drsophiayin.com.

CattleDog Publishing
P.O. Box 4516
Davis, CA 95617-4516
Email: info@drsophiayin.com
Fax: 530-231-5907
Phone: (888) 638-9989
www.drsophiayin.com

# Teaching Fido to Learn to Earn

Dr. Yin's Program for
Developing Leadership in Humans
and Impulse Control in Dogs

## TABLE OF CONTENTS

# A. Introduction

From excessive barking and jumping, to aggression and separation anxiety, one of the common issues is that these dogs tend to lack impulse control and their humans need to find better ways to provide guidance and leadership.

Fortunately, you can develop the needed communication skills while training dogs to have self-control and emotional control in one fun, reward-based program called the Learn to Earn Program. In Dr. Sophia Yin's fun, reward-based Learn to Earn Program, you gain leadership by controlling all the resources that motivate the pet and requiring the pet willingly work for play, treats, and pets instead of getting them for free. Now, the focus is all on using all valued resources to reward desirable behaviors while simultaneously removing the rewards for undesirable behavior.

This overall approach has been called "nothing in life is free," "no free lunch," or "the learn-to-earn" program. Each behavior consultant has his or her own variation. The following program is an overview of the Learn to Earn Program for Developing Leadership in Humans and Impulse Control in Dogs. This program is laid out in more detail with step-by-step photo-illlustrated instructions in *Perfect Puppy in 7 Days* (chapter 5).

# B. Overview

## B.1 Say Please by Automatically Sitting Is the Foundation Behavior

In this Learn to Earn program, the idea is to use everything your dog wants to your advantage as rewards for training purposes. The dog will learn to earn everything she wants by politely and automatically saying please by sitting. She will, at the same time, learn that performing undesirable behaviors, such as jumping on you, cause the potential rewards for those behaviors to go away.

For the fastest training, your dog should earn her meal throughout the day when you are home. That means no food in the food bowl. Instead, you'll carry food around with you in your pockets or a bait bag or have it available in easily accessible containers throughout the house. Then, throughout the day, when you are home, you'll reward appropriate behavior.

## B.2 How the Learn to Earn Program Trains Leadership and Communication Skills in Humans

This program consists of setting clear rules for your dog to automatically sit for all resources. You learn to communicate the rules by immediately (i.e., within seconds) reinforcing correct behaviors as they occur, and preventing your dog from receiving rewards for undesirable behaviors. So a large part of this program is learning the exact body movements and timing that help you convey a clear message.

As a result, this process is similar to learning to lead like a partner in dance. When partners dance as a couple, one leads and the other follows. The leader's job is to decide ahead of time which steps to perform and then guide his partner in a clear manner so that the partner CAN follow. Partners who have to shout out the steps or who yank their followers around don't make the cut.

With animals, the approach is similar. If you set rules and have a clear picture of what you want, you can consistently convey this information to your dog through your body language and perfectly timed rewards. Alternatively, when rules change randomly or the messages are garbled, your dog may view you the same way you might view an indecisive boss who mumbles.

Strive to set guidelines and communicate the rules by consistently rewarding desired behaviors and removing rewards for unwanted behaviors until the desired behaviors become a habit. At that point, your dog will see you as a leader whom she can trust to guide her.

With the Learn to Earn program, rather than complying out of fear, your dog will choose to follow your direction because doing so leads to rewards. Over time, following human direction becomes a habit. This model reflects a good understanding of the underlying cause of improper canine behavior and leads to a stronger dog–owner bond.

## B.3 How the Learn to Earn Program Leads to Self-Control in Dogs

In general, dogs have impulse control issues because taking things without asking, barging through the door, and pulling with all their might have worked so well in the past. For some dogs or breeds of dog, there may be a physiologic or genetic tendency towards having less impulse control, which means their humans must carry out the program more thoughtfully and consistently than owners of other dogs.

In this program, we turn the house rules on their head. Whereas taking things without asking worked before, the only thing that works to get him what he wants now is to automatically say please by sitting.

Start with easy situations, such as requiring your dog to sit for treats or kibble delivered by hand. This way, you can quickly build up a high rate of reinforcement, leading to a faster rate of learning. Next, systematically work with more difficult situations, such as sitting to play fetch or for the opportunity to chase squirrels. At that point you expect longer or more bouts of desired behavior for fewer and fewer rewards.

*A high rate of reinforcement leads to a faster rate of learning.*

### B.4 The Benefits: How the Program Changes Your Dog's Perspective

Because dogs learn that the only way they can get what they want is by sitting and looking to you for permission, the Learn to Earn program teaches them:

- to control their emotions (self-control), even if that means remaining calm.

- that paying attention to you and your words, signals, and guidance are important; it gets them what they want.

- when faced with a difficult situation, they can and should look to you for guidance.

Consequently, the Learn to Earn program is useful for dogs with fear, anxieties (including separation anxiety), arousal issues or hyperactivity, and inability to focus on their owners, as well as lack of training and unruly behavior.

### B.5 Why Training During All Interactions Throughout the Day and for All Resources, Including All of Their Food, Is Important

This training throughout the day and for all resources, including each piece of kibble, may seem a huge inconvenience, but doing so will make a huge difference. Here's why you do it.

- **So your dog will develop a habit rather than a trick:** If you only train in specific sessions, your dog may learn to behave only during those training sessions. The things you do at the start of such sessions, such as pulling out a treat bag or placing a special collar or leash on, will become the cues to behave for just that short time rather than behaving well all the time.

- **Because you're training your dog all day, during every interaction anyway:** Whether or not you're aware of it, every time you interact with your dog, you're either training your dog to behave desirably, or you're training undesirable behavior. For instance, if you reward your dog for sitting to greet you when you come home on day one and remove rewards for jumping to get your attention, yet, later in the day, your dog comes over in a less excited state and you pet her when she shoves her nose and then her front paws onto your lap, you're negating your earlier training because you're rewarding her for pushy attention-seeking behavior. That is, in one instance you're training her to politely ask to be petted; in the second case, you're training her that it's OK for her to push her way in. So whether or not you think you're training your dog all day, you are. **If you're unaware of what you're doing, you may be spending more time training bad behaviors than the behaviors you want.**

- **To get overnight success:** Because most dogs eat a least 100 pieces of kibble per day, if you're using the dog's regular meal as a reward, she'll get lots of rewards during the day and consequently learn the new behaviors quickly. That's because the higher the reward rate, the faster the dog will learn.

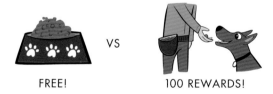

Then, if you add other resources, such as petting, attention, and play, when she wants these things, you'll increase your toolbox of rewards. Add to this removal of all rewards for undesirable behavior, you now have a formula for changing your dog's behavior patterns virtually overnight (meaning days to weeks instead of weeks to years).

- **Often when dogs are misbehaving, it's because they want a resource anyway.** If you're aware of what they want, you can use it to your advantage. For instance, if your dog gets overly excited to go on walks, meaning she jumps around when you want to put the leash on and then darts out the door, you can train her that the leash goes on only if she sits and she gets to go out the door only if she sits and focuses on you until you give her a release word. That is, while you may use quite a few treats at first, ultimately, for these behaviors, the reward is not food, it's getting the leash on and going out the door.

## B.6 The Necessity and Benefits of Tethering Your Dog to You at First

In the first days of training, your dog should be tethered to you on leash at all times when you are at home and she isn't in her crate or pen, dog-safe room, or tethered to an object near you. When she's not tethered to you, she specifically needs to be in some type of situation where she can't practice unwanted behaviors, such as barking, pacing, and others that reinforce poor impulse control. Tethering to you is especially important because:

- If your dog's near, it's easier to reward good behaviors as they occur. Otherwise you tend to forget and miss opportunities, which makes training take weeks or months longer.

- Because she's supervised, it's difficult for her to practice or perform unwanted behaviors.

- Tethering to you teaches your dog that when she doesn't want to pay attention to you, she can't just blow you off, walk away, and then get rewarded by something else, such as a dropped food wrapper. That is, tethering her to you helps prevent rewards for undesirable behavior.

I use a Buddy System hands free leash (www.buddysys.com) for tethering to me or furniture. I keep my dog on a regular flat buckle collar or on a harness that hooks to the front, such as the Freedom Harness®, Easy Walk® Harness, or WalkinSync®.

## B.7 How Long to Continue the Plan

Some people assume they'll have to continue this intense program forever. The reality is that **if you work at this diligently, your dog will make more progress in a week than most dogs do in many months.** For most problem dogs that I work with in my house, it takes just several days, or at most a week, for them to sit regularly for everything they want in the home situation. For more difficult dogs, this stage may last longer (3-4 weeks for me, which means much longer for you).

So that you know how long you will have to continue requiring your dog to automatically sit for everything she wants in the house, here are two rules of thumb.

- **Continue the complete indoor program, including tethering,** until your dog readily and automatically sits when she wants something—food, attention, to go out to the door—and any time you are stationary. In addition, continue until she comes 100% of the time when you call her in the house so that you can call her away from situations where she's likely to perform unwanted behaviors. To develop that 100% come when called, let her drag a long leash when you can supervise her and practice come when called frequently.

- **Continue the sit for everything,** even when your dog's behaved enough to be off leash in the house, until you have the perfect dog that you want. Remember that impulse control in one situation will affect arousal and control in another. If your dog goes bonkers over squirrels and tennis balls, say please by sitting in order to play fetch is important for getting him to behave well around squirrels, too.

## C. Implementing Dr. Yin's Learn to Earn Program (The First Steps)

### #1 First, teach your dog to automatically say please by sitting for treats.

- **Read** *Perfect Puppy in 7 Days,* **section 5.2 and watch videos at** www.drsophiayin.com with Say Please By Sitting in the title.
- **Training Dogs to Sit: Say Please By Sitting** http://drsophiayin.com/resources/video_full/say_please_by_sitting
- **Training Dogs to Sit: Say Please Part 2** http://drsophiayin.com/resources/video_full/say_please_part_ii
- **Training Sit: Say Please and Suddenly Settle** http://drsophiayin.com/resources/video_full/say_please_and_suddenly_settle
- **Training Sit: Stellah Learns Self-Control** http://drsophiayin.com/resources/video_full/stellah_sits_for_excited_petting

Hold a treat when you have a hungry dog (on leash) and quietly wait for her to sit. Once she sits, immediately give her kibble or treats, followed by a few more treats sequentially for remaining seated. Then take a few steps backwards, far enough that she has to get up and follow. Repeat the exercise 5-10 times, and stop while she still wants to play more.

Randomly play this repeat sit game during the day. The goal is that she thinks sitting is fun, and trotting after you and sitting fast becomes a game. Try to get 10 repeat sits in a minute. When she can do this easily, start rewarding her on a variable ratio where she may get rewarded every 1-3 times she performs the behavior correctly. For ways to make sit even more fun and compelling, read section 5.2.2 in *Perfect Puppy in 7 Days*.

## #2 During the day, keep her tethered to you when you're at Home (or to furniture close by when you're at home) and reward her for saying please until the behavior becomes a habit.

For many dogs, once they know the sit-for-treats exercise well, which usually takes just 5-15 minutes, they are ready to be tethered to you when you are at home in situations where they would have access to interacting with you. Tethering allows you to reward Fido with treats (kibble) for sitting repeatedly so that she learns that sitting and focusing on you is fun. If she tries to nudge, paw, or jump on you to get the treats, stand still like a tree and ignore her until she sits. For instance, if you're working at your desk and she puts her paw on your lap, immediately stand up so it's clear that doesn't work, then when she sits and looks at you, give her a series of treats. Or if you walk to the kitchen and clean the counters and she sits, reward her with a series of treats. As she improves, use fewer treats and space them further apart.

When your dog's attached to you on leash, she should sit and remain seated when you are stationary and walk by your side on a loose leash (not ahead of you) when you move from place to place. Choose the same walking side you use when you take her on walks.

If your dog tends to dash ahead, remember to always stop immediately as her front feet get ahead of yours, even before she has a chance to get to the end of the leash. That way, by the time she does get ahead, it will be clear to her that you have become firmly planted like a pole and are going nowhere until she comes back and sits in front of you.

Your dog's response after a couple of days to a week will provide clues as to how consistent you've been. If, when she hits the end of the leash, she comes back to sit and look at you, you've done a great job. If, when she hits the end, her first reaction is to pull harder, you know you've accidentally trained her that pulling gets her where she wants to go.

**NOTE:** If you can't easily get from one side of the room to another with your dog at your side in the house because he's pulling constantly or getting you tangled in the leash, you will need to practice the leave-it game in Step #4 first. You may also need to work on one or two heeling games (such as repeat sits on the left side and rewarding walking at attention) before your dog is ready to be tethered to you when you are walking around the house. Such heeling exercises are covered in *Perfect Puppy in 7 Days, How to Behave So Your Dog Behaves,* and at www.drsophiayin.com/blog.

## #3 Apply the say please by sitting exercise to the game of Leave-it version 1.

(For a more complete version of this exercise, read *Perfect Puppy in 7 Days* section 5.4). This exercise teaches the dog to 1) look to you for guidance in new situations, 2) that she can't get what she wants unless she asks you for permission anyway, 3) that blocking means she can't get by, and 4) that a release word such as "OK" means she can have what she wanted.

Toss a treat on the ground and block your dog from getting it. If she tries to make a dash for it, quickly sidestep (like a basketball player on defense) to make your block. Avoid grasping her leash with your hands (in basketball you're not allowed to grab!). Each time she makes a move, thwart her by positioning yourself in her path fast enough so that she knows you mean business. Because you're not confusing her with distracting chatter (e.g. you are completely silent), she'll figure out that she can't get to what she wants and will then sit and look at you. Immediately give her a treat while she's still sitting, and then give her a few more for remaining seated. When she's stably looking at you instead of the treat on the floor, move aside so that she has a clear path to the treat, but be ready to block her again if she starts to get up. Give her a series of treats for looking at you. When she's stably looking at you, release her with an "OK" and point to the treat to indicate that she can get up and get it. Repeat this exercise until she immediately sits and remains focused on you until you give the release (generally at least 5-20 practice trials).

At that point you can add a cue word "leave-it" right before you drop treats so that she learns leave-it means sit patiently and look to you for permission.

You can also start practicing in more realistic settings, such as by randomly dropping food in the kitchen or a toy in the living room, telling him to "leave-it" and blocking him if needed so he doesn't get it.

## #4  Add the leave-it game version 2.

In this version, you toss the treat out of leash range and then stand completely still. When Fido pulls to the end of the leash and you fail to budge, she'll soon figure out pulling gets her nowhere. Since she's been rewarded so much for sitting and looking at you, she'll turn back and sit in front of you. Give her a sequence of treats and when she has a stable "watch," say the release word and point to the treat. Make sure she can get to the treat on a loose leash or you will have negated what you just did. Note that this exercise helps teach Fido that when she gets to the end of her leash, she should turn and then sit and look at you.

## #5  Require That Your Dog Sit Politely for Everything She Wants

For more detailed instruction, read section 5.3 in *Perfect Puppy in 7 Days* or watch http://drsophiayin.com/resources/video_full/stellah_sits_for_excited_petting.

**Say please by sitting automatically to be petted:** This may be the most difficult exercise for you, because you may pet your dog without thinking about it. You may unintentionally reward the wrong behaviors if you pet your dog at the wrong time. The say please by sitting exercise is especially important for dogs that jump on people for attention or that are highly motivated for petting and attention and anxious when they really want to be petted. In this exercise, pet your dog only when she's sitting. Pet in 5–seconds bouts so that you can reward her for remaining sitting.

Remove your hands and stand up straight and look away if the dog starts to get up. For wiggly dogs, you can start by giving treats while simultaneously petting so that she will hold still, and stop petting and treat giving at the same time. Work toward petting followed immediately by giving treats before she starts to wiggle. Then pet her while you are giving her treats, but space the treats out in time. Then stop giving treats altogether and just reward with the petting. If your dog is really wiggly, hyperactive, or anxious, require that she lie down instead of sitting to be petted.

- **Say please by sitting automatically to get the leash on or have it taken off:** Wait for your dog to sit politely before you put the leash on. If needed, you can give treats while putting the leash on. If treats are needed, practice putting the leash on at least 5-10 times a day. That way, by day two or three, treats will no longer be required.

- **Say please by sitting automatically to go through door:** The leave-it technique applies to waiting to go through doorways. Instead of letting Fido rush past you, first wait until he sits to open the door. Then when you open the door, block him, as you learned in the leave-it exercise. Let him through the door only when he's sitting stably and focused on you.

- **Say please by sitting automatically to get out of the car:** If your dog loves riding in the car, and in particular getting out, then have her sit patiently before you let her out of the car. Again, use the blocking exercise to train this. Ultimately, the goal is to get her to sit automatically and wait for your release word without needing any treats.

- **Say please before you toss a toy:** When Fido wants to play fetch, wait until he sits to toss the toy to him. If he has huge arousal issues around toys, teach him to sit or lie down and remain seated even after you toss the toy. This exercise is particularly important for dogs that get more aroused and unruly during or after playing fetch and with those who are possessive over their toys.

- **Say please by sitting in order to get you to approach:** If your dog is overly dependent and whines or barks when you are out of her reach because she wants your attention, tether her to furniture and walk away. Approach and pet her only if she will sit when you are just outside of her petting range. When she understands this association, graduate to expecting her to sit if she wants you to approach. That is, you want her to learn that whining, barking, and howling do not work to get your attention. Rather, sitting or lying down and controlling her emotions is what gets you to approach and pet her.

These are the standard times when dogs should say please by sitting, but you should also tailor the "please" to your needs. There are other situations, such as coming out of the crate, where your dog must learn that he gets what he wants only by being calm and collected. Overall, these exercises will help your dog be calmer, stay more focused, and exhibit better self-control. As a result, he'll be able to be more attentive to your signals and directions.

**Conclusion:** That's the summary of my version of the Learn to Earn Program for Developing Leadership Skills in People and Impulse Control in Dogs. Once your dog has good focus and impulse control in the house, you can start building her focus and impulse control in increasingly difficult situations such as on walks, around other animals, when playing at the dog park, and whenever she is scared.

You can apply the same exercises to many situations where your dog acts on impulse instead of looking to you for guidance. You'll probably need to add a few more exercises that teach your dog that it's fun to stick by you even in high-excitement environments.

To see the detailed, photo-illustrated explanation of the exercises summarized in this booklet, read *Perfect Puppy in 7 Days: How to Start Your Puppy Off Right.* This book is appropriate for puppies as well as adult dogs and their owners.

For answers to common questions about this program, read the next section.

To see if you truly understand the concepts, take the Learn to Earn Quiz at the end of this booklet.

## Answers to Common Questions about Dr. Yin's Learn to Earn Program

**What if my dog is not "motivated" for his food? He'll eat it out of his bowl when he feels like it, but he's not hungry when I want to use food for training.** Dogs who get their food for free out of their bowls are often picky about when they eat—although most probably eat more than they need to and are overweight or obese. To get them motivated to eat when you want to use food as the reward, you have to make the resource more valued—limit its availability to build demand. If your dog's healthy and not interested in eating, then feed him less for a day or two. The rule is that he gets only what he's willing to work for (vs. giving the rest of the food to him for free!). Pretty soon he'll realize the free-food tree has dried up and he now has to start working for his keep.

**Can we have Fido loose in the kitchen with the family when we're not training him?** Every time you are with your dog, you are training him even if you're unaware of how. If he's free in the kitchen with people milling about, most likely kids or adults will be accidentally rewarding him for impulsive or pushy behavior. For instance, he may rub up against them and they could be completely unaware that they are responding by petting him. Behavior modification is more about training the humans than the dog. The dog can learn new habits in just days to weeks. Human error can drag the modification process out for months.

**What should I do if he jumps up to surf the coffee table or counter?**
Since he's on leash, you can easily pull him off. Do so swiftly (within a split second) so that it's clear the jumping didn't work. Then be sure to reward him a lot for sitting on the floor. At some point the light bulb will turn on—counter surfing doesn't work to get food, but sitting politely does.

**What if he is fidgety when I'm working at the computer or my desk and he's tethered to me or to furniture nearby? He's very active and tends to pace in the house the entire day anyway.**

Offer him a toy, even one that's edible, but that will last. When using edible toys, remember to factor the approximate calorie count into his daily allotment of food. You can also place him in his crate, a separate room, exercise pen, or even a yard as long as he's not practicing unwanted or anxious, overly aroused behaviors such as barking, lunging, and pacing. Later on, you can work on training him to lie down calmly while you work, since he does need to learn to be calm anyway. An easy way to do this this, which also allows you to get work done at the same time, is to use the MannersMinder remote controlled reward training system (http://www.youtube.com/watch?v=BDOiJsjaLTA). The MannersMinder can also be used to help train your dog to be calm in his crate, when separated in a room, and when outside in the yard.

Manners Minder

**How about exercise? How should I exercise my dog?** At this point in the game, when you're focusing on the indoor exercises and your dog has not yet developed fantastic focus inside, you can take Fido on walks the way you normally do. Later, once you've worked on heeling exercises in the house and have good focus, you can focus most of the training outside. Other alternatives to outdoor walks include playing fetch in the yard or treadmill exercise. You may need to teach your dog to play fetch first. (http://drsophiayin.com/resources/video_full/how-to-train-a-dog-to-play-fetch). Realistically though, while exercise is important, when your dog learns that impulse control and calm behavior gets him what he wants, he won't need to be worn out through exercise to behave calmly and politely.

# Dr. Yin's
# **Learn to Earn Quiz**

Your pooch is on Dr. Yin's version of the Learn to Earn Program that's summarized in this booklet and detailed in *Perfect Puppy in 7 Days*, so you are familiar with the program. But do you know the concepts well enough to get the fastest results?

**Test your knowledge here.** »

**1. What percentage of meals should be fed in a bowl, and what percentage should be used for training?**

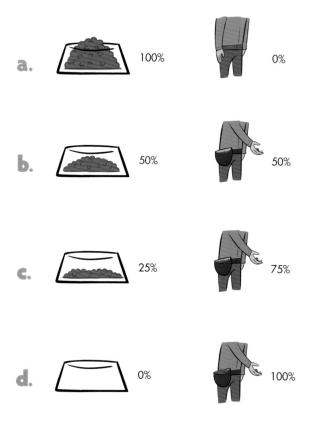

a. 100% 0%

b. 50% 50%

c. 25% 75%

d. 0% 100%

**Answer:** D: 0% in the bowl, 100% used for training. For fastest training of new desired habits, use 100% of the dog's meals to your advantage in training. Carry portions around in a vest or bait bag so that you always have them when needed when you are with the dog.

**2.** In addition to food, which of these motivators should you use as rewards?

**Answer:** Rewards are A, B, D, E. Use what your dog wants at the instant you are training as a reward for the behavior you want. Throughout the Learn to Earn Program, use everything your dog wants as motivators or rewards for good behavior. In the situations depicted above, the dog is focused on the owner for petting (A), praise (B), toy (D) and getting her leash on (E), the owner should require the dog to sit for these things. In situation C, the dog is sitting but does not care when the owner pets her. The dog looks away, so petting should not be used here because it's not rewarding.

**3.** **When you are not actively working on rewarding good behaviors and removing rewards for unwanted ones, where should your dog be?**

a.

b.

c.

d.

---

**Answer:** B, C, D. When you are not actively working with your dog and are not in a situation where you can be certain you will not reward unwanted behaviors or give away rewards for free, your dog should be set up so that she's somewhere where people cannot accidentally interact inappropriately with her and where she will not practice unwanted behaviors. For instance, she can be in the yard with a few toys (even a chew toy as long as you factor that into her daily calorie allotment), but not if she will practice fence fighting with other dogs or barking at passing cars.

**4.** The Learn to Earn Program teaches your dog that she gets what she wants in the house only when she says please by sitting and looking at you (dog pulls to get to toy, you wait until she turns and sits, you tell her OK, she gets toy). Circle the situations when this will help outside.

**Answer:** All of the above. By training your dog that sitting and asking permission gives her access to things she wants in the house and yard, you are priming her to learn the same lesson outside on walks. The better she's learned the rules in the house, the more easily she can learn to generalize once you apply the home exercises to the new situations.

## 5. Which is correct and which is incorrect?

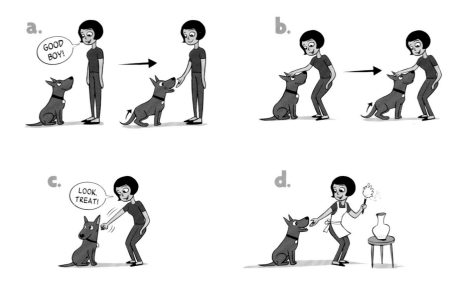

**Answer:** Incorrect: A, B, C/Correct D. When rewarding your dog, give the reward while your dog is performing the correct behavior. So if you reward (with treats or petting, such as in example A) while the dog's starting to stand up, you are rewarding the standing motion. The reward serves to reward everything up to the point that the dog is rewarded, not just the one behavior that occurred right before. So some dogs specifically learn to sit and then get up rather than to just sit. When you use a reward that your dog doesn't care about, you are not are not training effectively (example C). Stop the training session or move to a more effective/appropriate motivator.